OTHER BOOKS BY TRACY PORTER

Woven in Sunlight: A Garden Companion

Returning Home: The Poetics of Whim and Fancy

MINI BOOKS

Gentle Influences: The Spirited Ties of Sisters

The Journey Within: A Book of Hope and Renewal

TRACY PORTER'S
Dreams from Home

WRITTEN WITH DEBORAH HERNANDEZ AND ANN PORTER
PHOTOGRAPHY BY KATY ROWE AND DALE STENTEN

These are my thoughts this is my language

Andrews McMeel
Publishing

Kansas City

www.andrewsmcmeel.com

98 99 00 01 02 TWP 10 9 8 7 6 5 4 3 2 1

Library of Congress Cataloging-in-Publication Data

Porter, Tracy.
    [Dreams from Home]
    Tracy Porter's dreams from home : these are my thoughts, this is my language / written with Deborah Hernandez and Ann Porter ; photography by Katy Rowe and Dale Stenten.
        p.   cm.
    ISBN 0-8362-6773-7
    1. Porter, Tracy—Themes, motives. 2. Interior Decoration. I. Hernandez, Deborah.   II. Porter, Ann.
III. Title.
NK2004.3.P67A4   1998
747'.092—dc21   98-6436
                                                                                                          CIP

ATTENTION: SCHOOLS AND BUSINESSES

Andrews McMeel books are available at quantity discounts with bulk purchase for educational, business, or sales promotional use. For information, please write to: Special Sales Department, Andrews McMeel Publishing, 4520 Main Street, Kansas City, Missouri 64111.

Acknowledgments

For those who came, saw, conquered, and contributed I thank you.—THSP

Chris Schillig—"Ala Allah" The All seeing, All knowing, All telling—We're not worthy.

Dorothy O' Brien in her ruby red slippers, thank you for skipping down the yellow brick road with us.

Polly Blair, thank you for your wisdom, wit, and wonderment.

Deborah Hernandez, aka Truman Capote/"Derby" Terrio

Sarah Willett—Chief Rectangle aka Nest on Plaid

Katie Rowe and Dale Stenten, thank you for peeking into our looking glass.

Denise Randolph, "Stylist extraordinaire"

Matt with the Magic Touch Sherwood

John Sparky "I'm in estrogen hell" Porter

Christine "Scary Doughnut with the Glittered Rack" Phillips

Jodie B'Goadie Radar Ferguson

Jean Meyer and Tricia Krumbein, Artists extraordinaires

Dave "Skinny Dippin', Salmon Makin', Martini Sippin'" Schaberg

Annette "Feast Makin', Antique Collectin', Shakin Bakin' Momma" Schaberg

Robyn "I'll just sit here and be pretty" Schaberg

Courtney "Keep those grades up, Smarty" Dille

Amanda "Hopscotch, Willy Nilly, Tick Tock, Be Silly" Dille

Grandma Lucy—We miss you.

Ann "The Grammar Hammer" Porter

Margo "Follow your Bliss" Brown

Paul "I'm happy that Easter is in November" Brown

Katie and David "We're here for the food" Porter

Billie "Gee, Candy is dandy" Sieracki

Maura "How can you stand it?" Koutoujian

LeAnn Sieracki, thanks for Billie

Pam "Earth Angel" Doherty

Fiona Doherty—Our ethereal ringletted nymph

Lily "Fairy of the Cake" Stenten

The Poodles and the Princesses: Abby, Caroline, and Chris Wilson; Lily, Kylie, and Monica Barrie

Lydia Randolph—Queen of the Ball

Bob Brenner—The king of holiday

Ann "Where did you get those window boxes" Mijatovich

Deb "Freeze frame" Fletcher

Conrad Naparella—Your sixty-six splendid years of life on our farm graced us with a most wonderful first home. Thank You.

Matt Lind—Professional tulle hanger

Our entire team of artists and enthusiasts

Rodeo Jack—Fastest Donkey in the Midwest

The dogs: Sir Walter Periwinkle—The wondrous Weimy

Otis, The cheese-loving Bulldog—Cheese!,

Higgins McGee—Wiener Dog! "Sorry,"

Alcott "You're such a peach" of a Redbone Coonhound

The city of Princeton, Wisconsin—Thank you for having us.

Contents

Dedication

For Deb and Sarah, two of my dearest friends whose never-ending efforts helped make this book and every day a fantasy journey.

For my husband, John—Je t'aime toujours.

For my family, whose constant encouragement and love have allowed me to be a free spirit since childhood.

For my brother, Danny, who assured me ten years ago that my paper, scissors, and glue would never fetch me a career. (KMA) ♥

COTTAGE AND GARDEN—Cottage, yellow with white trimmings; Roof and Roof of Porch, red; Door, dark green; Curtains, blue; Window Boxes, dark green; Flowers in Boxes, red with green foliage; Chimney and Paving at Front Door, brick red; Flowers in Garden, red, yellow, blue, and lavender; Hedge and Bushes, dark green; Grass, light green; Distant Trees, light green; Sky, blue with white clouds.

I was sitting on the painted floors of my sun-filled living room with the remains of children's scrapbooks, coloring book pages, and school projects found in the attic when we moved into our new house. Sorting through the remnants of the childhood lived by the former owner of our 103-year-old stone house. As I sifted through the tattered remains of a stranger's childhood memories, I discovered a crudely colored illustration instructing the way a house should be painted. Doors: yellow. Shutters: blue. Roof: red, etc., etc. I sat for a moment pondering the very idea of "should be." Anyone who knows me well understands that "should be" definitely goes against my grain. Too limiting, too predictable. Not fun, not innovative, and certainly not expressive! And besides, "should be" doesn't work when you are experiencing home ownership for the very first time. A first home symbolizes freedom—mine was decorated by a farmer who remained a bachelor for over seventy years. This new house was an opportunity to experiment with our environment, and it was an amazing and challenging project.

For John and me, life in the country brought new experiences to our very new marriage. This recent move was reminiscent of my childhood growing up on a gentleman's farm in Fond du Lac, Wisconsin. Twenty-five years later, as I wind my fingers around the handle of a small bucket and feed grain to my own animals, I am sent back to those mornings in the past on Artesian Road.

For my husband, John, well let's just say that each day here at Stonehouse Farm brings a new adventure. It was the day after Christmas in 1991 when John and I abandoned our urban cares and fled Chicago in pursuit of a rural, idyllic life. In Chicago, we had collaborated on the very beginnings of our own small business. Our goal was to make and sell the most beautiful hand-painted wares in the world. (No small feat, as we later learned). Ever since I was a kid, I've been making things: herbed candles, paintings, jewelry, beaded handbags, hand-painted furniture, mosaics, découpaged treasures, felted projects —you name it and I've probably tried it. Early on, others knowingly advised me to "narrow my scope," or "focus on doing one thing well." The variety of my experiments was an unparalleled education on the way things are made, better preparing me to design for our business, Stonehouse Farm Goods. John loves to tell tales of my adventures with an acetylene torch in the basement of our Chicago row house. My unthrottled passion drives my enthusiasm for home and making pretty things. Everything about the process of creating excites me!

3

We happened upon Stonehouse Farm after several unanswered phone calls to a variety of local real estate agents. The agents just didn't seem to understand that we were not only ready to buy, but we were also starting our life and a sensational new business together. The first requirement for our desired farm was a long and winding driveway. Outbuildings would be a plus, because we needed an artist's studio for the new business. The property of our dreams needed a pasture that was ideal for farm animals, and the house, quite frankly, was an afterthought. So much so that, after walking the twenty-one acres for the first time with the agent, John and I turned to her and exclaimed in unison, "We'll take it!" The agent replied, "Folks, do you think you might like to see the inside of the house?!"

"Somewhere I have never traveled gladly beyond any experiences . . ." A quote I love because it says that there is an expedition out there just waiting to begin! I love a good journey. Bienvenue!

Deciding to move to Princeton wasn't solely based on a return to my roots—it was also an escape from the city. Don't misunderstand me; I love the city. My years in Chicago provided me with tremendous opportunities— diversity, shopping, museums, jazz clubs, dancing, endless sights and sounds, and (most importantly) amazing food! Yet the years I lived in Chicago also gave me an outrageous mortgage, seventeen keys on my key ring, traffic jams, a glove compartment stuffed with parking tickets, the reality that parking spaces didn't exist anywhere near my home, and a genuine fear that each morning my vehicle would be blessed with the Chicago Police Department's "Denver Boot."

All things that are most magnificent to me are tattered by age and glisten with wisdom.

The baubles that marked the beginning of our new life. A chandelier given to us by my parents. Lucky us!

Many beloved objects find their way to the collection on my dresser. I love the ritual of arranging and rearranging precious objects in a special setting.

Perhaps we believed that no matter how bad the house was, we would figure something out. John had dabbled in some rehab projects back in Chicago and I had a knack for creating spaces on a shoestring. Besides . . . how bad could it be? What we found was that it could be bad. Bad, beyond our wildest dreams! There were seven space heaters just on the first floor, dark faux paneling in every room, who knows how many layers of linoleum hiding the most amazing hardwood floors, low ceilings, shag carpeting throughout in a rainbow of colors, and a living room that was to be transformed into a local nightclub and bingo casino! The list of godforsaken imperfections was endless, but we were too excited to be daunted by the colossal challenge in front of us. Besides, at that point in our marriage the one thing we had plenty of was time on our hands. Our current state of unemployment, with hopes and dreams of a new business, didn't exactly leave our pockets overflowing. It was time to get to work. With our families help we made the move to our new Princeton home on the day after Christmas, 1991. We began by stripping, scraping, and ripping up all unwanted surfaces, followed by sanding and smoothing. From the floors to the walls, countertops to cupboards, we attacked with all our youthful vigor. Since all our resources went into our new business venture, we used whatever was available for the house. Paint was the obvious answer to our dilemma, and we used it everywhere that you can imagine.

People visiting our quirky stone house are greeted by doors painted with galloping animals, floors of dainty plaids and bold harlequin, bathroom tiles masked with paint, and kitchen counters rubbed with color, découpaged, and then sealed with a resin coating. These may seem like unconventional treatments for renovating a house, but we lost our heads to the process of embellishing! In that first month, John and I found ourselves in the midst of the American Dream and lost in the rhapsody of creating our home.

The future belongs to those who believe in the beauty of their dreams.

—Eleanor Roosevelt

Relying on furniture we dragged from the alley behind our city apartment, hand-me-downs from everyone we knew, and flea-market finds, we set up house.

That first year we combed estate sales and auctions all over Wisconsin in search of rickety treasures we could afford to transform for our beloved nest. What we didn't find, we designed for ourselves and hoped to sell through our new entrepreneurial endeavor.

When it comes to a philosophy of living, I've been accused of wanting to have my cake and eat it, too. Well, of course I want that—doesn't everyone? Having the best of both worlds is the best situation imaginable. I love not having to compromise. Perhaps this is how I've come to incorporate such diversity in my style. I need to have some of all of it. More is definitely more. The best options are always win-win. The challenge is in pushing yourself outside of your perceived, predetermined "box" and creating your own destiny or style. My style is driven by passion; whatever trips my trigger becomes part of my signature. I refer to this signature style as American Rhapsody. Having the city and the country, simplicity and chaos, small business and big impact is all about what appeals to us. Warning: It may take more effort, creativity, and resourcefulness to determine your own fate.

Now, outside my front door I have a sanctuary provided by nature and a spirit within. This haven encompasses the ideals of what I believe in and what I seek out of my existence. It's a far cry from life in the city, yet just as exciting in my eyes. John and I live here and work here and play here and love here. Our life certainly isn't perfect, but it is a life we have personally created and we want to share with others.

P.S. What is truly exciting about a win-win existence is that it's possible.

Fiddleheads—an original work of art created in the studio at Stonehouse Farm. I am constantly amazed at the delicacies that grow in the wild pasture; earthy mushrooms, spindly stalks of asparagus, and wonderful curly fiddlehead ferns. Each year at the farm brings a new discovery.

Of BLUEbirds anD BaTs

THE Imperfections of CHarm

I don't want a house that
has got over all its troubles;
I don't want to spend the rest
of my life bringing up a young
and inexperienced house.

—Jerome K. Jerome

To me, a home is a fantasy waiting to be revealed. Things are so rarely perfect. As soon as we accept this fact, true living can begin. Unfortunately, many home owners want the picture without the flaws. They fight the imperfections instead of appreciating them. This philosophy may help to explain our delight in living in an old house with more than a few shortcomings.

On first sight, anyone would have been hard-pressed to believe that Stonehouse Farm could ever be the fruition of our fantasy. The front yard was buried under an array of lawn ornaments and broken-down farm equipment. There were more poles and wires running across this property than on our entire city block. From the ancient windmill in the center of the yard the spokes of electric lines splayed to all points of the compass. And inside what a sight to behold!

Our floors? Slanted. Our ceilings? Unbelievably low. With a touch of disgust mixed with sheer disbelief and not a little bit of delight, I describe them by saying, "I can palm every ceiling in my house!" The walls? Okay, let's just say that what wasn't covered in brown paneling looked like the pocked, irregular surface of the moon (pictures and mirrors keep my secrets). The bathroom? Almost functional and as deep and wide as a bathtub. The kitchen? Perfect, if you don't mind a sink that backs up, counters that induce back pain, and electrical wiring that sends your husband flying (isn't that right, John?).

Despite all of this, the house was blessed with several amenities—nice doors, ample closet space, a spacious dining area, a mud room, and an abundance of delightful nooks and crannies. It's an odd and quirky house,

but it is ours. John and I were thrilled to have our own canvas on which to experiment and dare, adding another layer of character to the house with the objects of our desires. A chandelier in our guest room looks as if many hands have tried to alter its surface, clay pots rubbed with rust and dirt look as if they were unearthed centuries ago, while a weathered, paned window frames a delicious handmade collage. These shards of rusted, worn, and damaged elements are brought together to create a thing of exquisite, even sophisticated, beauty.

To spice up the exterior of the house, we added gingerbread to the eaves followed by a white picket fence around the front garden. Turned wooden posts and railings were added to the porch. Inside we chose our battles by priority. A bookcase covered walls that were cracked and unattractive while providing places for our many books and favorite collections. My crooked dressing-room floor was covered with fabric, braced to the floor with tacks. With paste and time, I papier-mâchéed our bathroom floor with paper leaves, concealing the mold that lay underneath. These small projects enhanced the cleverly painted walls to create a look and feeling that is our own. The satisfaction is all ours, the rewards of hard work, best enjoyed in moments of leisure.

Since I cherish my time at home, I've had to let go of any yearning for perfection. As much as I try, there is always dog hair on the couches, hay scattered sparsely on the floor, scratches on the furniture, and cat hair on our clothes. I take comfort in a home that is cozy, warm, and welcoming to all who visit. Guests may dance in our living room. A spilled drink isn't a disaster, just an excuse to refill the glass. Every Easter, our families play a vicious card game of

Spoons on our dining room table. I don't wince each time a spoon slides across the table; instead I pray that I'm not left sitting without one. I love our home for it is truly lived and loved in.

We were recently discussing a wish list for the house, and John said that the stairs needed repainting. In a split second I blurted a horrified "No." I couldn't imagine covering up the years of memories contained in our steep and winding stairway. I painted them six years ago and as time passed, the layers have peeled away. The original red paint is beginning to show through and the memory of our home is coming alive. Looking back, I remember furniture that had to be hoisted through second floor windows because the staircase wasn't wide enough. I think of our dogs, Gilbert and Alex, carefully and deliberately climbing each step to the security of sleeping at our sides. No, the stairs will stay for some time yet.

One of my greatest inspirations comes from being surrounded by all that I love—our home, our animals, our business, our friends. To look out of my studio window every day and see the beautiful expanse of land that envelopes our home, and to watch Judge, my horse, holding court with all his witnesses: the sheep, the goats, and the miniature donkey, Rodeo Jack; to live, work, and play in such an environment, I'll take imperfections in my home any day.

Whether your home blesses you with bluebirds, bats, or both, try to appreciate its charms and flaws. I believe it's most often the unlikely, quirky, whimsical things about a home that make it so enchanting. If not, we are left with white canvases that search endlessly for true breaths of life.

It's all about finding the diamonds in the rough!

Create your own American Rhapsody by letting go of the baggage that can hold you back. Let go of your:

FEAR—OF ANYTHING, BUT ESPECIALLY OF MAKING A MISTAKE. REMEMBER, THIS IS YOUR HOME; WHAT FEELS GOOD TO YOU IS WHAT IS TRULY IMPORTANT.

Expectations—It's okay that you can't recreate every beautiful idea you've just seen in your favorite home-decorating magazine (or in this book, for that matter). Check the inadequacy thing at the front door and play up the things that you love about your place. There is a reason you are standing in its midst. What is it you loved most about your place the first time you laid eyes on it ?

Rules—Time to unbuckle the safety belt. It's the mix, not the match. What you love, not how it goes with what you already have. Just because you love traditional doesn't mean you can't have a quirk or two! Just let go and have fun.

Blank canvas syndrome—Where do I begin? How do I start? By the way, this syndrome also falls under Fear. What you need is inspiration. Let something influence you. It doesn't matter if it's as simple as a color or a favorite piece of furniture that must be a focal point in a room, or as complex as creating a decorating wish book. Whatever it may be, fine, just get going!

What about these photos will you never see?
A. A gaping hole behind the picture
B. Paneling in the hall
C. Gray formica countertops?
D. All of the above

13

Her name was Lucy

The story of a Peacock

As I ponder the things I love about designing and creating a home, I realize that I'm drawn to and influenced by so many different forces. Family is a major and essential priority in my life. My siblings and parents have certainly helped to shape me as an adult, as did the experience of having my grandmother living on my parents' farm. Her home on our property became my childhood destination, my great escape. Every evening, I would slither away from after-dinner chores to nestle in the warmth of all that belonged to her.

My grandmother was many things, but first and foremost she was French. In the course of sixty years living in the States her accent never diminished. Lucy was very French and very proud—redundant, of course. Not much here in the States ever quite measured up to her standards—the food, the art, the clothing, the pastries, or the perfume. She shared endless tales of her life in France, taught me French words and songs, and enlightened me about the culinary habits of her revered France. I adored my grandmother because in her aloof way she intrigued me. She was not your typical doting grandma, but was, in fact, quite direct. When she wanted to she spoiled us rotten, but she could be tough as nails. Very French!

Character is higher than intellect.

—*Emerson*

My grandmother's red velvet sofa became my favorite place to sit during our nighttime visits. Thoughtfully passed on to me on my wedding day, this generous gift will forever remind me of the woman I held so dear. Her treasured belongings have added splendid character to our home. Although many of her possessions are hand-made, their refined quality reflects the care that my grandmother took in her meticulous hand-work, and the love that she had for fine, extra-ordinary things.

Her modest home was filled with the most savory treasures. If there was half an inch of ricrac left from a dress she had trimmed, she saved it for someday. I vividly remember her linen closet. She had treasure chests full of wonderful French fabric remnants, velvet millinery flowers, delicate trims, bric-a-brac, and intricate lace. And she could make anything! Delicious pastries or tedious beaded hats with feathers, crocheted blankets and tailored jackets. I believe much of the detail that I add to my art and home stems from the world I discovered in Lucy's closet. I learned that my grandmother had an impeccable style and a remarkable knack for living quite a charmed life. She made each little gathering special and memorable. Food was always prepared with the

utmost care. Its presentation included lovely serving trays and small adornments like a petite bouquet of flowers or a sprig of herbs. Cloth napkins were a must and nothing short of immaculate table manners was tolerated. I adored her for every ounce of attention she showed me and admired her constant state of grace. As children, we just don't realize the impact of our family experiences—I guess this is one of life's precious lessons. These are the cherished memories of my grandmother that provide me with great inspiration. We are often so busy with our harried lives that we forget to take the time to truly enjoy life, to pay attention to the details that make it all worthwhile. My grandmother held dear the simple things—the feathers of a peacock, a spool of pretty ribbon, a beautiful cloth napkin, a homemade dress, and most importantly, time with loved ones. An avid animal lover, like the rest of my family, Lucy loved birds

of all kinds. Her favorite was the exotic peacock, and there was one in particular that captured her heart, a pet she loved more than life itself. Years later my grandmother sent me a peacock at Stonehouse Farm as a housewarming gift. A common trait of this flamboyant bird is its habit of wandering, and so it was with our new peacock after just two weeks in its new home. Our beloved bird vanished into thin air.

My mother made me promise that under no uncertain circumstance would we reveal this situation to my grandmother, for it would certainly break her heart.

Every time we visited her she inquired about our lovely bird and how he was getting along. Reluctantly, I shared many tales of this gallant peacock and his adventures at Stonehouse Farm. My mother was determined to shield my dear grandmother from the truth, and much to my surprise, she'd chime in with tales sometimes taller than my own! This gentle charade was repeated for years, since my grandmother lived to the ripe age of ninety-six.

One month after the sad and inevitable day of her passing, a very strange thing hapened. It was early evening at the farm and the chickens were making their way back to the coop for their night feeding. At that moment, I looked out the window in disbelief. A very large peacock was making his way up toward the chicken coop as if he had just discovered his new home. I was thrilled to see the magnificent creature strutting among his new feathered friends. Excitedly I reached for the phone. As I heard my mother's voice on the other end of the line I could barely whisper through my tears, "Mom, you'll never guess who's here."

What dwells in our memory may fade, but the token reminder is forever potent.

—Deb Hernandez, my dear friend

AND BABY MAKES

Our animals complete the idyllic setting of Stonehouse Farm. Their comical, charming displays grace the spirit of our home, bringing with them a delightful bit of chaos. But more than creating the scenery of a picturesque view, the animals have inspired my ideals, paintings, and designs, providing the essence of what I imagine a home to be. We celebrate their vitality and invite them to make their humble place in our world. The sight of a sleeping dog stretched out on a bed of heirloom pillows, or the cat who lies in slumber on a bed of freshly washed linens, is for me an affair of the heart. Our animals enhance our lives as a constant reminder of spirits that are innocent and free, their energy constant. You will find fragments of their beauty throughout our home, from the collection of antique farm animals discovered while traveling through the flea markets of London, to the exotic animals bounding through jungles pictured on the panels of our doors. When I make my way up to the house each evening, I'm greeted by rabbits, chickens, geese, and ducklings happily awaiting their evening treats. Once inside our mud room, I'm surrounded by the evidence of our pets—weather-beaten grain buckets, Judge's tack and saddle, now worn to perfection, baskets filled with dog bones and biscuits, and an abundance of cat toys and treats. The responsibility is awesome; the fullfillment is complete: Their inspiration is infinite.

Who loves ya, baby? At the end of the day there is nothing like one of these dear hearts to keep you grounded and smiling.

10.

OUR MENAGERIE

Our stone house revels in the personalities of our domestic animals. The first to the farm were Amelia the calico cat, whom we've spoiled since our days in Chicago, Spike, our rescued alley cat, and Alex, a Norwegian Elkhound, John's first venture into animal husbandry. Their love of the farm was exceeded only by ours, and they were the beginning of what has become the "Porter Menagerie."

John, I'm sure, never pictured his life as being filled with morning chores. Oh, there are plenty of responsibilities, from deworming sheep to, you guessed it, shoveling horse manure. Yet we fell in love and mutually agreed to find a home in the country where he would, indeed, be required to do such things. On my first birthday at Stonehouse Farm, John showered me not with fine jewelry or exquisite clothing, but with the most incredible gift of three pregnant Jacob ewes, Aily, Annie, and Laverne. Our dream of living and working together on a gentleman's farm had truly begun.

The animals are a part of every aspect of our lives. They are the first
thing we see out of our window in the morning; they follow us to
the studio, settle into our artwork, and bid us good evening at day's end.

Following the arrival of the pregnant ewes, we were blessed with the gift of a horse. What do they say about looking a gift horse in the mouth?! Judgment Day is our five-gaited saddlebred and he was a most welcome addition to the farm. When Judge arrived he was skinny, scared, and quite difficult to handle. Today he is the dominant ruler and faithful protector of all of our animals at Stonehouse Farm and, to be honest, better looking than any day he ever showed in the ring. Three sheep and a horse quickly became fifteen sheep, a goose, a horse, a pygmy goat, a miniature donkey, and a rooster named Clyde, as well as several chickens, rabbits, and ducks. The domestic lot has grown to include a female Akita pup named Gilbert and a soon-to-be-born Newfoundland. You can never have too many loved ones.

Convinced as we are that the animals keep us humble and grounded, each addition to our family brings new duties and lessons. We learn discipline as the last animal is fed at dawn in the bitter cold February air, and loyalty as the animals make their way up the pasture's hills each evening to receive their treats. They humble us daily, whether we are performing not-so-loved chores or witnessing one of the sheep give life to a new lamb. Yes, it's true: the animals provide for us.

The animals are, of course, quite dependent on our care; they have come to expect their daily feedings, waterings, and treats. And as much as we like to believe that we're in control of our days here at the farm, there's no doubt that the animals actually call the shots. No matter what may be happening in our busy business lives, the animals and their agendas are priority one. John and I, as witnessed by our management team on several occasions, have fled the studio midsentence to investigate one of the animals that appears to be limping toward the barn. We have rescheduled many a production meeting around our sheep shearer's schedule, put off design brainstorms due to the arrival of the baby miniature donkey, and even rushed out to the pasture to rescue Annie, of the original Sheep Trio, from a burning barn. On many days, everyone at our studio can watch me try to trap the ever-cunning Judge moments before the arrival of the farrier. Sometimes, it seems that we are actually living in a comedy directed by our animals. Or as John would say, "It's their movie—we're just lucky to have a bit part."

Lest we ever forget our faithful companions!

25

How sweetly did they
float upon the wings
Of silence through the
empty vaulted night,
At every fall smoothing
the raven down
Of darkness till it smiled!

new twist of combining patterns, delicious candies, patterns that dance, restful white spaces, glistening tea cups, the texture of moss, the color of sea animals, the gentle scent of a springtime flower. Just a bunch of nonsense? Or perhaps the closest thing to a formula that I can offer as explanation of my design process. I'm not particularly fond of Keep It Simple, Stupid. If I'm not researching and discovering then I'm most likely bored. The "Simon Says" theory certainly doesn't allow any freedom of expression. But if you pack an open mind, you just might discover there is fresh perspective to be found, even in the rules. Be brave, shake it up, break rules, ask questions, and have some fun!

I am fascinated with questions, asking them of others and answering the ones that people most often ask me. Where do you find inspiration for so many pieces of artwork and for designing so many things? My inspiration for creating a lifestyle and business comes from many directions. It thrives on evolution. Like a great big, round magnet rolling through the world picking up anything that sticks. The magnet keeps getting bigger, allowing me to borrow from it for each new challenging project. I don't have a formula for how I draw inspiration, I just go for it. I guess you could say that I'm a bit of a fanciful, curious rebel. Society sets us up to maintain the status quo, but it's up to us not to be brainwashed. Asking questions lets us avoid the traps.

I can be a bit nudgy. I don't like to get too comfortable; I keep pushing and challenging myself. Staying out of the comfort zone is what American Rhapsody is all about. It's not just inspiration for designing pretty things or decorating a home—it's a way of life. Daring to go beyond the tastes, smells, sights, touches and sounds that one is used to. Throwing away security, forcing yourself to try new things, taking different paths and constantly changing directions. If we don't experiment we won't grow, and growth is what makes life so delicious!

There is, of course, a method to my madness, although for years I avoided having others label me. That unbearable 'box" that would sum up my art, thought process, and being. I want to change all of those as often as I like. After some time I realized that if I didn't define myself, then others would do it for me. And many times their interpretation can be pretty far off. It's always better to be the director than the one being directed.

Inspiration is about aesthetic instinct, you must trust it before you can convey it with confidence to others.

Inspiration exists in everything around me. What I do is about the whim of combination, the color that creates a statement—I just make the selection. I can even borrow from what I dislike. I find myself evaluating and learning to sift through my design process to get to the core. I don't ever want to get into a rut when I'm designing so I try not to develop an actual system. If I approach creating a piece of original artwork, a new design, a display for our store, or a vignette in my home from a different starting point each time, I'm confident that the idea will be original.

Limitations can force you to be more creative. When John and I first moved to Stonehouse Farm, we were strapped by starting our new business let alone decorate our first house. In the midst of expanding our line of hand-painted furniture, I always held in my mind the colors I wanted to paint the interior of our home. Tansy, Sage, Meadowlace, Cerise, Caracas, and Miss Willoughby became the familiar color names for our Stonehouse Farm Goods, as well as the hues that filled our nest with it's first layer of warmth.

There are no big secrets to creating a home. Sometimes it feels good just to take a risk! Add an element of surprise. In my crooked stone house there is a winding staircase that leads to the second-floor bedroom, guest room, and bath. With its intriguing "green as a lime" staircase, the hall sets the stage for the unexpected. (It's a little wicked to be unpredictable.)

"You go ahead, Tracy, and you take your scissors, paste, paper, and crayons and you go find yourself a career."

—Tracy's brother upon her decision not to go to college.

To believe your own thought, to believe that what is true for you in your private heart is true for all men—that is genius.

—Emerson

I love games and play them often when I'm designing. You should hear the words buzzing in my head as I flip through magazines and my favorite tattered old books. "Okay, in the next ten pages I will find five things that inspire me." And just like that, I do. A simple exercise like this may send me down twenty new roads of combining colors. All of a sudden, this twisted perspective renews my process and my designs take on a fresh face. Creative exercises can be applied to our lives—even routines can vary. One of the Girls told me the other day that she pulls five magazine tear sheets every weekend to inspire her wardrobe for the coming week. She claims that this exercise saves her from standing dumbfounded in the closet each morning. No time is wasted and she has fun with the normally routine and mundane. A simple way to break out of the box!

Keeping a dream book is one way to keep files of inspiration. Dream books can be filled with anything from insightful quotes to intriguing tear sheets. Fashion and beauty tips, home ideas, garden references, or travel magazines, dibs and dabs like buttons, ribbon, and fabric remnants, antique post cards, pages from worn books, and cherished notes are all gleaned from my many sources of inspiration and secreted away in my dream books. Whether used to spark the memory of someone dear, decorate a fantasy room, or inspire my wardrobe, a dream book keeps the muses at my fingertips.

Here is an exercise that I do: If a room in my home needs a face-lift, I find at least five things I can add that give it new character. A favorite bowl from the kitchen becomes a soap dish for the bath. An Adirondack chair from the front porch keeps summertime in the living room all winter long. Turning favorite fabric remnants and ribbons into a delightful photo trellis for the bedroom sparks keen memories. Stacking books in a new way, out of the bookshelves and onto the dining room table as a base for a centerpiece, enlivens dinner conversation. Assembling a variety of objects of the same color against a brightly painted wall changes the scene. Transforming the garden shed into a wonderful open-air studio for the summer months will refresh the spirit. Make a space. Dedicate a room in your home for something special: a space to create, pot and sow your garden seeds, read and reflect, be peaceful, or exercise and grow strong.

Dare yourself to try something new. In the studio, we keep lists of words and sometimes use them to simply inspire new displays at our retail store. A word, a place, a color, or theme gives us the perfect focus to recreate a new store presentation. This same exercise can be applied in a room that you'd like to reinvent. Perhaps today you want to live in the South of France. Okay, go and gather all of the things that conjure thoughts of Provence—a tattered piece of lace, a rustic table, fresh produce displayed in a colorful ceramic bowl—and assemble them in the room of your choice. Recreating an environment with what you already own is the easiest, most inexpensive way to give your place a lift. Walk through your house and find a few objects that have never been moved from their current place, and find another appropriate space for them. Perhaps there is something that lives in your garden like a cloche or a gate that could bring a hint of the garden indoors during the winter season. I have a wonderfully weathered screen door that lives year round in my hallway.

One of my favorite childhood games was Truth or Dare. I loved the dares for their excitement and unpredictability. I disliked it when someone chose truth. What big, bold secret did any ten-year-old have to reveal? Boring! As adults, however, we are more apt to take the truth rather than the dare because we've learned to conduct ourselves in a certain way, as we always have, without risk.

The things that count: startle yourself with color, defy gravity and your expectations, persistently contradict yourself.

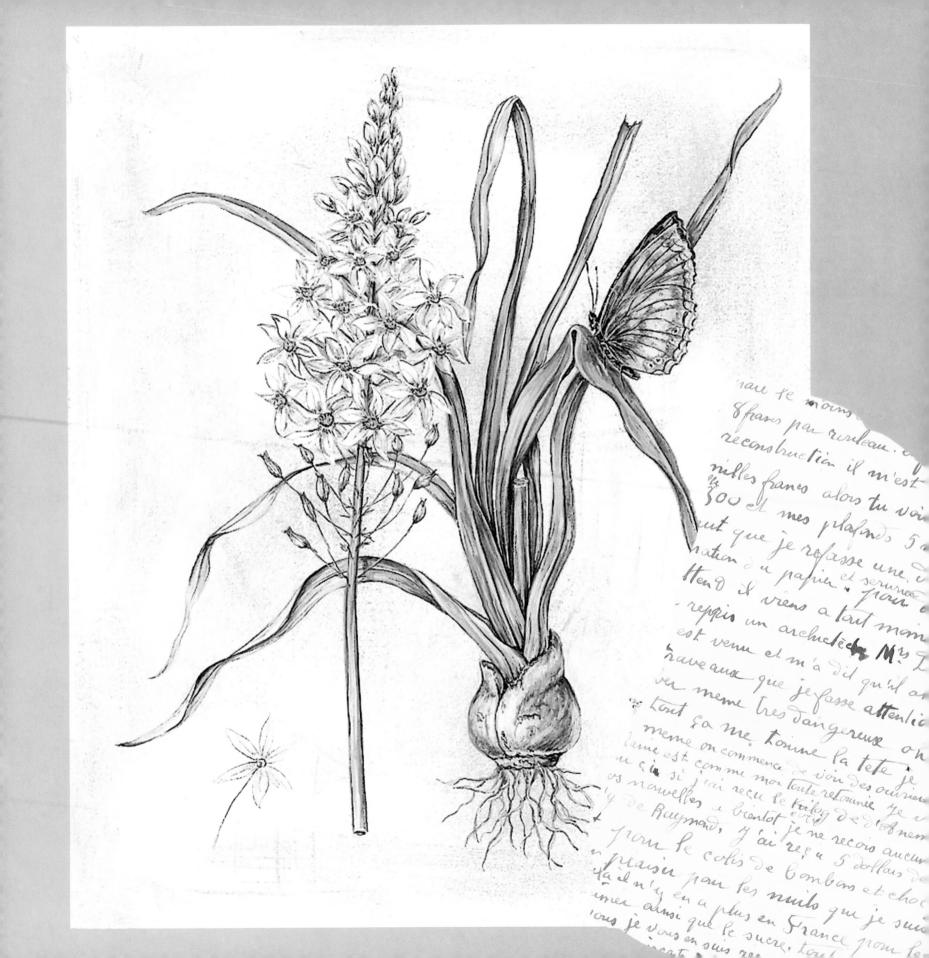

Country on all four sides...
Living in the middle of nowhere

"The middle of nowhere" is often the way we describe this particular area of rural Wisconsin. Not quite close enough to a major city to qualify for errands on your lunch hour, unless of course the errand is picking up grain for your farm animals. In that case, there are two feed mills just a stone's throw away. Most errands like dry cleaning and shopping for organic produce require at least an hour's drive. After a restful weekend entertaining friends from the city, they usually ask the same question, "But what's it really like to live here? I mean . . . like, year round?"

Well, that leads to an interesting observation about a desired way of life. For us, the contrast works. Just because we live in the country doesn't mean that our fascination with glorious food, eclectic taste, eccentric decorating and fantasy entertaining must come to an end. In fact, just the opposite is true. Seek and ye shall find! Starting with home, the opportunities to borrow from our surroundings are endless.

35

Let the seasons inspire you. Bring some of the outdoors in or even better, create an indoor room outside. We moved one of our most elegant tables outdoors and plopped it right in the center of the garden. A winged angel bearing gifts of the season made a gorgeous centerpiece and my rustic chairs were layered with moss, leaves, and fresh petals. Simple but elegant dishes laden with brie and sliced figs made a wonderful late afternoon snack for a visiting friend. An experience to relish. Imagine the scene on a crisp fall day nestled amid tall pines. The effect changes completely.

Wherever you live, let your surroundings embellish your lifestyle. Don't ever feel that you have to give things up. Whether it's strawberry picking in the spring, growing sunflowers on a city rooftop, adorning a mantel with nature's treasures, or discovering a fragile bird's nest that becomes a centerpiece for your table, look at life as an opportunity to try things on.

I want my home to feel like an amazing journey into a colorful world—a world where one might expect to see things differently. So many of the perfect little extras that make our home imaginative were discovered right in our backyard. Delectable fruits and the splendor of flowers indoors help us celebrate the vital spark of nature.

Sanctuary in the nest during the winter months. Sanctuary free of the nest in summer months. Winters are long in Wisconsin. After many days with the fire roaring and windows tightly sealed, I'd give anything for the sweet scent of lilac or the heady aroma of freshly cut grass. One late spring afternoon, I decided to transform our front porch into a reading nest. I dragged my exquisitely worn living room rug to the porch, followed by a favorite wicker rocker and fanciful ottoman. For privacy, I encouraged my overgrown vines from the garden to act as my curtain while one of my favorite framed images hung from the branches blowing freely in the breeze. I gathered dripping candles, a rusted wire sconce, my most prized candleholders, a cut crystal vase bursting with ochre yellow flowers, and a hot cup of tea. On my last trip indoors I loaded up with stacks of wonderful books covered by a throw made of Italian textiles. My private place to hide, surrounded with beauty and the comforts of my farm in the middle of nowhere.

Was it a vision, or a waking dream? Fled is that music— do I wake or sleep?

—John Keats

Whether we live in the country or the city, "the garden" touches all of us. Perhaps a fresh topiary rests on the mantle, or maybe a bowl of English lavender naturally scents a guest bedroom or bath. Herbs started indoors before making their way outside. A forced bulb in winter or drying cut hydrangea blooms. If you have tried any of the preceding ideas, then it's official—the gardening bug has bitten you. In every way, the garden is meaningful.

A wonderfully battered hoosier cabinet houses my garden essentials. It's the only place my crumpled, dirt-embedded gloves and Wellie boots can call home. Over the years, my gardening tools, books, and pots resemble a collector's lot much more than that of a weekend gardener. In the dead of our cruel Wisconsin winters, my potting shed stands guard faithfully as a reminder that spring will indeed come again.

I find the garden both soothing and rewarding. I have no expert advice to give; just learning while doing. The reward is in the growth of a sprout, an arrangement of homegrown flowers or the nothing-quite-like-it taste of a summer tomato. Sure, I'll pass along a gardening tip or two to friends, but mostly I work by trial and error. Stick it in the ground and see what comes up. Weeding isn't at the top of my priority list. In fact, my love of an overgrown cottage garden satisfies the "more is more" in me. My philosophy: The more you plant the less you notice the weeds! What I love most about a garden is its evolution. Mine may be unpredictable but it grows better every year.

It's delicious like green cheese.

Living in an eclectic environment

What does it mean to be eclectic?
Sometimes it means you are room wise
and space-foolish, but mostly it means,
"Sure, throw it in. Why not?" If you
follow your own intuition, you'll
find domestic bliss—really, you will.

44

Freedom is a condition
of the mind, and the
best way to secure it
is to breed it
Elbert Hubbard

American Rhapsody is the result of our hearts' desire. It's about everything that we do. "American" is obvious, and important. Believe in your individuality, freedom of expression, pursuit of happiness, seek and you will find. Entrepreneurial spirits and opportunities abound in this country. Brave adventurers and tenacious pioneers of new frontiers forage food for thought; we all want a piece of somewhere else to feed our inspirations. Revel in the fortunate abundance of what freedom really provides. Making the decisions, having the options, determining the selection—the sweet tune of exercising choices is the music that keeps playing.

"Rhapsody" provides the emotion. Exultation and enthusiasm are the necessary attitudes. Rhapsody describes my work and its signature style: unusually intense and somewhat irregular. I sum up its inspirations as a jumble of the spontaneous and impassioned miscellaneous. American Rhapsody is the symphony heard when climactic drama meets sensuous harmony.

Live Your Passion! This is one of the many mottos I use to deny any predetermined boundaries for living. Allowing our passions to drive us provides the ever ready road map for our lives. Passion sets goals in the subconscious. No need to labor through a rational thinking process—passion naturally leads you to incorporate your loves into your life. John and I make food a definite priority. If food is one of your loves, keep tasting and experimenting, and before you know it you'll develop a finely tuned palate.

To live your passion is to treat yourself every day. Passion can be a constant positive force that moves you daily. What could be better than this? I live with what I make because I only create what I love. This seems so simple and yet when I speak to other designers and creators they are sometimes baffled by my environment. Do I really live with the things that I design? I can't imagine why I wouldn't. Living with true passions keeps the harmony in our home. Perhaps this is why John and I break so many rules in our business life, like working with family and friends. Big no-nos, right? Wrong! Life is sweeter and richer when who and what you love is woven into your everyday pursuits.

Go somewhere and explore! Travels may take you down the road or to the other side of the world, but you'll always find along the way an opportunity to explore new places and new destinations: to find treasures. Let a passion to explore help you discover all of what life has to offer.

It's the mix, not the match! I apply this philosophy to the people I love, the objects I desire, and my designs. Anything can work together if there is a harmony about it. By harmony, I mean something special. A Chinoserie vase filled with old-fashioned flowers, a zebra-skin rug on a country pine floor, a chandelier from a Chicago mansion hanging in a stone farmhouse. Harmony has nothing to do with being expensive or authentic. It has to do with emotion. It makes you smile. It makes you laugh. It reminds you of someone special. It makes you want to touch it and look more closely at it.

Melding the many flavors of home is a delicate art, and there can be magic in the madness of your mixture. Take liberties and pursue originality, let your own eyes be your guide. For me, each project begins with the whim of play and finishes with a noble achievement. The artistic journey is my cake—I don't just eat it, I devour it with passion. Feeding my soul with the peaceful contentment that nourishes my dreams of home.

THE PASSIONS ARE THE
ONLY ORATORS THAT
ALWAYS PERSUADE;
THEY ARE, AS IT WERE,
A NATURAL ART, THE
RULES OF WHICH ARE
INFALLIBLE; AND THE
SIMPLEST MAN WITH
PASSION IS MORE
PERSUASIVE THAN
THE MOST ELOQUENT
WITHOUT IT.
—LA ROCHEFOUCAULD

Do the unexpected; tickle your imagination. "Eclectic" is frequently used to describe my rhapsodic style. In the past, I felt that defining my niche was something I couldn't do. It seemed too much like limiting my philosophy because I'm drawn to a wide range of styles. What I later came to realize is that I have a look but it tends to be mixed —the ever-present element of surprise. There is no one way that's "right." I live to love, discover, and challenge; these are the powers that drive me each and every day.

When I consider the possibilities for decorating a room, the finished project is not necessarily the goal. All the rooms in my home continue to evolve in the same way that my designs evolve. I keep my mind open to the many delights that thrill me, and I continue to add touches and transform my surroundings. This is what I refer to as Perfecting the Art of Puttering. Covering a tattered old lampshade with moss, using a stack of books as an end table, or a sprig of velvet flowers as a tieback for curtains. What I create makes me feel fantastic for the moment, but I know myself. The inevitable feeling of sameness will set in and I'll want to create a change. Living in a house that continuously changes adds another form of life and character to my home. So the goal is not to be finished, but to be on a never-ending journey, adding newly discovered treasures to my home's collections.

Individualism is rather like innocence; there must be something unconscious about it.
—Louis Kronenberger

More is more. This is the effect I love the most. I may need a "resting place" from time to time, but for the most part, just keep it coming! Layers, textures, colors, and patterns make me a little wild. Once I get going, it can be hard to stop. Perhaps that's why I love découpage and collage—you never need to stop! I love it when someone tells me there are no limits to the colors we can create and use. Wow! This is music to my ears and I can create from the best possible place. No limitations. This is when life is truly most sweet!

American Rhapsody—Eclectic Elements to Enlighten

1. Cover crummy floors with plywood and paint over them. Use fun patterns like harlequin, stripes, gingham, or plaids.

2. Pull out your silver- and stemware and show it off, perhaps displaying it as part of your permanent collection of books.

3. Cover an uneven floor with heavy upholstery fabric. Nail it in place with a variety of upholstery tacks.

4. Paint your hallway a shocking color and see if it helps you experiment in other rooms.

5. Create a collage on your wall with photos, love notes, bits of wisdom, elements of the garden, and any other favorite things.

6. Hang in Vain. Display or hang several miscellaneous mirrors on a wall in your bedroom.

7. Cover your light-switch plates with unusual materials. How about silk? Candy corn? Buttons? Corduroy? Small pebbles? Velvet? Moss?

8. Try découpaging a wall that's covered with hideous wallpaper. Instead of steaming and scraping, start layering over it. Gather your favorite pictures, quotes, photos—even color—photocopy some of your favorite images, gift wrap or fabrics.

Life is hectic. Not a big news flash, just an observation about our lifestyles that's more and more of a reality each year. It is, therefore, so very important to create a sense of wonder and romance in the midst of our harried lives. John's thirty-fifth birthday was the perfect opportunity for me to engage my imagination and invent a different way of marking an important milestone in the life of my beloved. I wanted to create a celebration that would be remembered. The setting had to be unusual, unsuspected, and undiscovered. The mood, magical.

In our five years at Stonehouse Farm, John and I had never quite addressed the task of cleaning out the silo. It occurred to me that this mystical, eerie, unexplored building would be the perfect stage for the grand event of John's birthday. Here was an opportunity to transform the ordinary into the extraordinary. Planning the evening became just as exciting as the actual affair.

It's practically impossible to surprise someone you live and work with every day. Beyond that, John is very observant and difficult to fool—not to mention that I am, without a doubt, the world's worst liar. I had to rely on invaluable resources to help me with my secret mission: The Girls.

I believe that true romantics try to create a new and better world far from the mundane routine of everyday life. After sending John away to help a friend, The Girls, Sarah and Deb, my cohorts in work and play, aided me in my quest. In a few short hours, we magically transformed a dirty, abandoned silo into an imaginative, glorious setting reminiscent of medieval times.

Join us for an Autumnal Supper

Autumnal Supper

Harvest Soup
Cornish Hens
Vegetable Terrine
Patty Pan Squash
Herbed Russets
Wild Rice over
Mesclun

Spiced Cider
Red Wine
Bountiful Cake

I love the contrast of a formal setting and the ease of our gathering. Once we're set, we are set. Time to forget about the preparations, relax and enjoy. We have been known to get a little out of hand!

Food whether fancifully
dressed or plain and simple
is still the best excuse for
the sound of conversation
and laughter exchanged
between family and friends.

A good cook is like a sorceress
who dispenses happiness.
                    —Elsa Schiaparelli

Annette's Squash Soup

1 Large butternut Squash ~ peeled, Seeded and cut into Chunks. aprox. 2½ lbs.

3 Apples ~ peeled, cored, chopped
½ cup chopped Yellow onion
1 garlic clove ~ minced
1 Leek chopped
1 ~ 49½ oz can of chicken stock
1 tsp. cinnamon
1 tbsp. brown Sugar
1 tsp. ginger
1 tsp. cumin

Sautee onions, garlic and leek until Soft in 1 tbsp. butter and 1 tbsp. Vegetable oil. Add the remaining ingredients ~ bring to a boil, then reduce heat and Simmer ~ covered for 45 minutes. blend in a food processor or blender until Smooth ~
Salt and pepper to taste.

Serve in a Small pumpkin or Squash.

Our plans for the enchanted evening were incredibly ambitious, but step by step we laboriously accomplished our tasks. We started with a traditional list of necessities for a birthday party—invitations, birthday cake, presents, menu, table setting. Our plan was to twist the traditional essentials into unique fantastical creations.

The evening's lavish feast had an autumnal theme and was served on a round table draped in silk and candles set with a mix of ornate, tarnished antique silver. The meal was carried into the silo on hand-painted trays covered with fall motif, on silver dishes embossed with acorns and twisting leaves, and on platters rimmed with pinecones. My collection of miniature wildlife animals pranced around our festive banquet table, authenticating the woodland scenes.

I like a fantasy setting that real people can experience. It's like a mysterious experiment. If this design thing doesn't pan out, I think I've got a shot at being a scientist. To create your own reality, you must know how to use the lab.

John Porter as the guest of honor. There is much to love about this man—he's up for anything at any time, drives like Steve McQueen, and can be the perfect gentleman. Watch out for the wit though, it's razor sharp! Trust me ladies, Chivalry is not dead.

Instead of a standard invitation, an artistic collage beckoned our guests. The cake was decorated with gifts of the season: glittered leaves, petals, and butterflies. Presents were not just wrapped, but embellished. A hot glue gun can turn a wrapped present into anything you fancy. For whimsy, we wrapped packages with sheets of moss, flower petals, plaids of ribbon topped with flowers made of leaves, miniature animals grazing on a pasture of ribbon, buttons, and berries. The possibilities are as endless as the imagination.

The warm glow of dozens of votives illuminated the silo, while a soft bed of corn husks, grain, and straw rustled underfoot. A rusted metal chandelier was wired with glittered leaves, tiny gourds, and pumpkins. Moss, pinecones, and berries were added and then the chandelier was lit with tapers.

"The following evening we sat hushing each other in the cavernous, dark silo awaiting the arrival of our guest of honor, like baby birds anxiously waiting for Mother to return to the nest. Silently like characters in a surreal play, wearing *Alice in Wonderland* character masks, and then the silo door opened. The flock of wild birds took flight!"

It's important to note that such grand happenings don't necessarily occur often at the farm. But after a magical night, we are certainly encouraged to reinvent our traditional celebrations with elements of fantasy.

The most beautiful thing we can experience is the mysterious.
—Albert Einstein

The taste of the Land

PICNIC IN The pasture

What better way to transform your everyday life into something special than a picnic? Picnics don't have to be the grand events that take place in backyards across America on the Fourth of July. They also don't have to involve packing up the kids in the family station wagon and driving for

hours to a remote location. The joy and delight of a casual picnic can happen simply in your very own backyard.

A visit with dear friends is the perfect opportunity to host everyone's favorite American pastime. Our cabin fever had the best of us and we hoped that this late spring

day would be perfect for an outdoor lunch with our guests. This would not be just any picnic, but one that reminded us of another feast last February, tucked between luscious olive groves and vineyards on a hillside in Tuscany. Once again our travels inspired our journey at Stonehouse Farm.

73

We searched within the walls of our home and dragged many of its comforts to our outdoor setting—the feed cart filled to the brim with pillows, blankets, candlesticks, neck rolls, small rugs, and throws. We wanted to be nestled in the comfort of a lazy afternoon nap. Such an environment also gave the only child present the priceless option of tumbling and bouncing about in the safety of comfy cushions and blankets. Like being given permission to jump on the bed, our friend's two-year-old daughter, Fiona, screamed with delight as she leapt like a bunny on her makeshift sofa from one pillow to the next.

We settled under a large, impressive oak tree in the valley of our pasture. This spot also happens to be one of the places the animals love to graze.

Today, however, the members of our menagerie were passive observers of a new event taking place in their usually private domain. Fiona's shrieking laughter rang out, and the animals became increasingly interested in this nymplike creature. Judge, holding his usual court, hesitatingly decided to investigate and join us in our afternoon escapade.

Antipasta

1 cauliflower broken into flowerettes
1 green pepper (1" cubes)
1 red pepper (1/4" strips)
3 celery stalks (2" sticks)
12 baby carrots cut in quarters
1 C. green olives pitted
1 C. black olives pitted
1 jar cocktail onions
1 can artichoke hearts (quartered)
7.3 oz. jar button mushrooms
1 can baby corn
1 can water chestnuts
1 large can albacore tuna

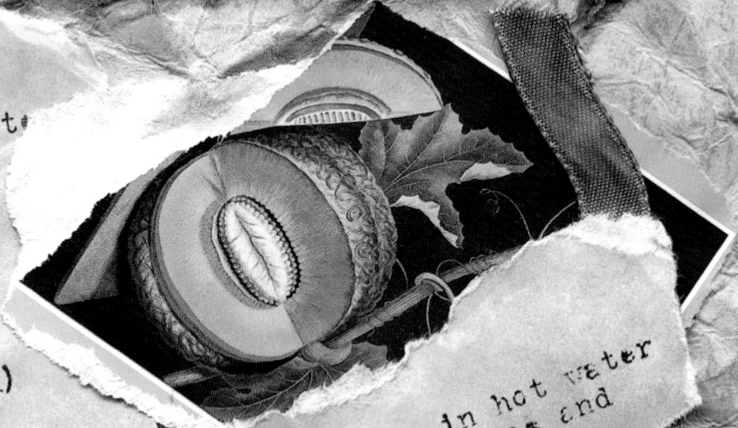

Blanch all fresh vegetables in hot water
for one minute. Cool in ice cubes and
cold water, drain.

59. PARIS — La Conciergerie   C. M.

Lucy's
recipe.

Sauce

2 cans Italian tomato paste
1/4 C. chili sauce
1/4 C. ketchup
1/4 C. cocktail sauce
1 Tbsp. olive oil
2 cloves Worcestershire sauce
1 Tbsp. minced garlic
1 Tbsp. lemon juice
salt and pepper to taste
white wine vinegar

Combine all sauce ingredients and mix with
drained vegetables and remainder of ingredients.
Chill 6 hours to develop flavors.

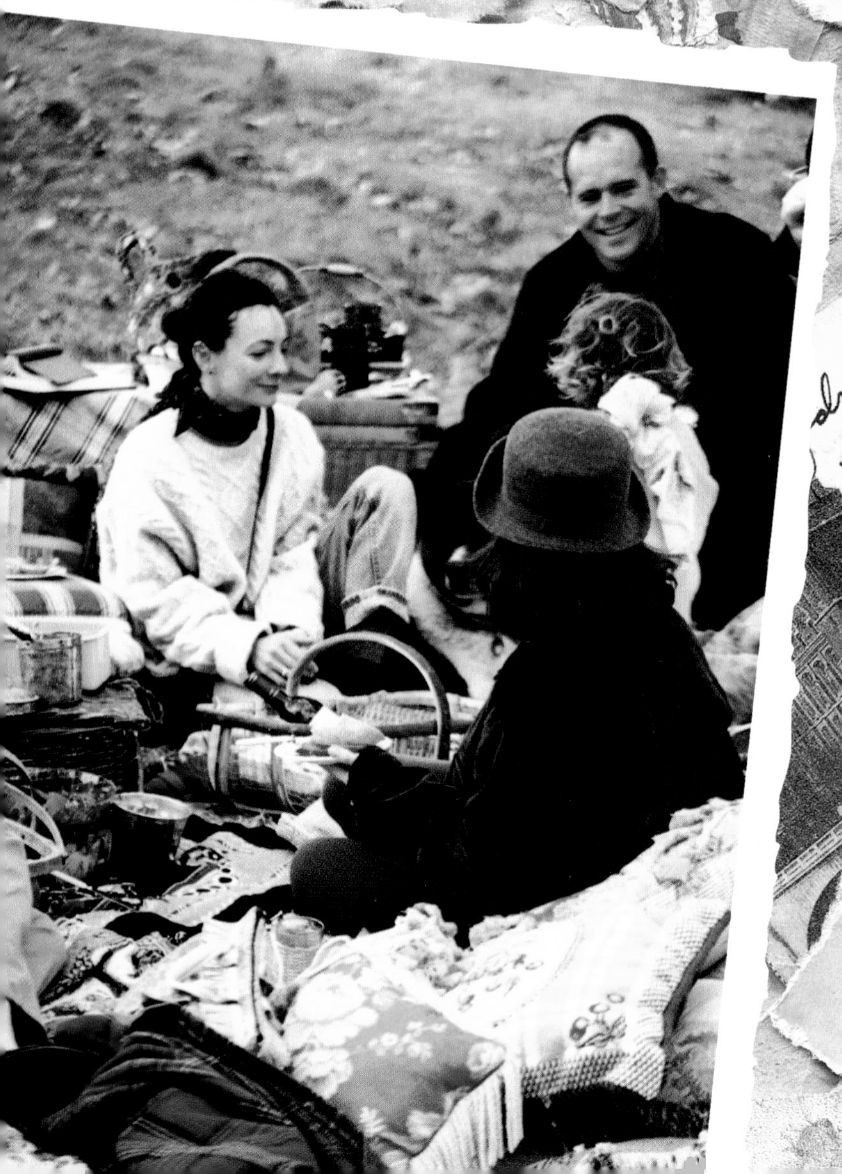

The most important aspect of our ritual, of course, was the food. Because our picnic was meant to be informal, the menu resembled that of our casual Tuscan spread. I love a meal when I can nibble and try a little of this and that. John and I are extremely casual with our friends. If everyone isn't kicked back and making himself at home, then it doesn't feel right. Everyone indulged the succulent roasted red peppers dripping in olive oil, marinated Meditteranean olives, and an abundance of Grandma Lucy's antipasto served with fresh herb garnish of flat-leaf parsley. A melange of favorite stinky cheeses graced both our plates and our nostrils. It's my personal belief that the closer a cheese smells to a horse's hoof, the better its actual taste! All the while, red wine was passed and glasses replenished. And for the grand finale, dessert, usually the first section of the menu that I scan, was an unbelievably rich pecan tartlet. When it comes to dessert we go rich or we don't go at all!

Packing-up the picnic Basket
Essentials for the Day

1. Butterfly Net

2. A Good Pair of Skates

3. Bubbly Champagne

4. Your Best Friend

5. Posies

6. Comfy Slippers

CHAMPAGNE DE MARQUE

7. An Antique Fan

8. Pixy Dust

9. Your Lover

10. Seeds for Scattering

11. A blue Unicycle

12. Delectable Treats

olidays in our house are all about fun. The first question I ask myself is how am I going to achieve a little bit of fantasy with not a lot of time and without spending a lot of money? The fact that I'm such a pack rat relieves a good deal of the pressure since I'm constantly collecting little goodies that I can use for different occasions. I find that with a little bit of planning and several months' worth of dime-store treasures, I can usually add a festive layer to my home. The last thing I want is stress when planning a gathering. If its not enjoyable, then there's really no point. Mostly, I like to wing it by opening up a closet and peering into its contents for inspiration. I love hunting and digging through candy aisles at places like Walgreens and looking for cheap craft stuff with embellishment potential at the Ben Franklin store. Listen, don't forget that I live in the middle of the heartland—not exactly the world of convenience, but the challenge keeps me on my toes. When all else fails, I hit the local indoor flea markets in search of some good junk. This process usually leads me to plans for table settings, gifts, menus, invitations, etc.

For our last Easter celebration I let my senses guide me. The smells, sounds, tastes, and sights of the event had to be absolutely delicious. The table setting began with a centerpiece stolen from our sleeping garden. A plaster pediment, a miniature glass conservatory, and a planter brimming with fresh grass and brightly colored Easter eggs filled the scene. I love a centerpiece that is not just a thing but an assemblage of the festivities. Liberate the tabletop and keep adding whatever layers that can be found. My table was scattered with penny candies, chocolate rabbits, jelly beans and Easter grass found at the local variety store.

Instead of a traditional basket, we decorated a huge grapevine wreath that resembled a very large bird's nest. The colossal nest was decorated with ribbons of springtime plaids, playful ricrac, dried hydrangeas, paper butterflies, and hand-painted Easter eggs for each of our guests. Maybe next year the nest will be transformed into a centerpiece for the table or used as a place to hold presents under the tree at Christmas.

The setting of the table is where I tend to get carried away. Because I'm not particularly fond of matching, I rarely have a complete set of anything in my home. Even the tableware that I designed myself is used in a mixture of patterns— My constant excuse to keep adding to my collection. I usually find some kitschy little gift for my guests—for Easter it might be a frosted wafer wrapped like a bonbon in tulle and candy confetti.

Tons of votives illuminate the Easter vignette set on a round serve-yourself table. My collection of rabbits have found their way to the serving table posing gracefully in their pastures of Easter grass and jelly beans. A copy of the enticing handmade invitation is placed in the vignette along with holiday cards and treasured childhood books.

Plates are laden with hand-made cornucopias. Each glittered cone filled with a nest of Easter grass and candy. A fanciful whim adds grace to the setting.

Recipe for Russian Cream

1 c. sweet whipping cream
1 c. thick sour cream
3/4 c. sugar
2 tsp. plain gelatin
1/2 c. cold water
1 tsp. vanilla

Add sugar to sweet cream in top of double boiler and heat until luke-warm. Add gelatin that has been soaked in the cold water. Stir until gelatin is dissolved. Remove from heat and cool when it begins to thicken. Fold in sour cream that has been beaten smooth. Beat mixture, add vanilla, and pour into molds to set.

RED WINE IS THE DRINK OF CHOICE IN OUR HOME, NO MATTER WHAT IS SERVED. MY SISTER-IN-LAW KATIE RELAXES WITH A GLASS OF WINE OVER EASTER DINNER CONVERSATION.

Easter Menu

Tarragon Salmon
coconut couscous
Asparagus w/ orange & sesame
Mixed greens & heart of palm salad
artichoke hearts with mirepoix
Russian cream (grandma Lucy's recipe)

An artful menu captures the essence of an Easter feast,
and the final course is most important. This time, it's
Grandma Lucy's Russian Cream.

Happity

bunny trail

Down

Easter is on it's way

We all know that children are most thrilled by what's in the trick-or-treat bag, the Christmas stocking, or the Easter basket. But imagine how magical that experience is when the basket is as exciting as its contents. Decorating Easter baskets is another excuse to get carried away. I love them fanciful with lots of ribbon, flowers, and bows, padded with Easter grass, moss, or colored tissue and then wrapped with clear or lustre celllophane. Each layer of celophane contains a new treat: paper confetti, penny candies, or glitter. Or collect plain containers throughout the year that can be embellished for each Easter treasure. Strawberry baskets woven with ribbons, wicker baskets fitted with vintage floral fabrics, or a wallpaper-covered hatbox make great goodie bags!

My Easter vignettes lead us through the house, to the most likely spaces that our guests will grace. Spring flowers in the bath are surrounded by candies, and Easter eggs are displayed in a baby bird's nest. A paper dragonfly teetering on top of a hallway mirror, and soap resting on fresh blades of grass sprouting from a tea cup hold moments of pleasure.

The Porter tradition begins with a toast before each holiday meal. Every meal John takes a different approach. Some toasts are witty and some somber with thoughts of those who no longer join us for these joyous occasions. Most are filled with our fondness for celebration and the opportunity to share a smile. John always ends on an upbeat note as we let the festivities begin.

There isn't a better time to have a fantasy party than in the dead of winter in Wisconsin. January casts a frozen spell on our days, icicles hang from the trees like immobile limbs, the sky is ashen with a haze of cloudy white, and a quick freezing rain puts our entire world under glass. It's the only time of year when color abandons us. We must be satisfied with the green pines until June. Sounds dismal, n'est-ce pas? Well, it's actually a very peaceful time. A time when a cup of tea and good books are satisfying and an afternoon nap is just a sofa away. Even in the winter, we can all infuse a touch of color into our days.

The first step in turning a dreary winter afternoon into passionate living was the concoction of a party with some of our favorite little girls and their dogs! We don't need a reason for celebration and fun, just fanciful thoughts and the spirits of any age to enjoy the festivities. We decided to host a children's party for the sake of color. To be completely honest, the hosts of this party don't even have children, but we definitely enjoyed watching their outbursts of delight.

Here is our gameplan as it unfolded, and it's surely our best girly-girl extravaganza to date. Well, this is actually the only one we've had to date, but one thing is sure—winter will be rolling around again.

Peace, Love, and Pastries

A fantasy tea & tartlette Party

93

Please come to a
Tea and tartlette party

bring your dog.....

94

O ur cast of characters had the time of their lives dressing up and playing make believe. Amanda as fancy lady, Caroline as the Twenties flapper, Abigail as lounge singer, Billie in her more-than-floor-length gown, Kylie as Hollywood starlet, one Lily as a dancer and the other as a sugar plum, and Fiona as Fairy Princess with wings. The little girls felt their costumes were incomplete until they layered themselves with jewels, scarves, hats, and gloves. Pack rats like myself and mothers of little girls often have plenty of delicious costumes on hand.

What makes our life colorful, anyway?
My list looks something like this:

The silly giggles of children
A pantry full of linens
Exaggeration
A palette of paints
Happy dogs
My favorite candy
Music that makes you want
   to dance
Fringes and frills
Wisconsin in August
   (only eight more
   months . . . gulp!)

Gypsy pattern
Impromptu occasions
Turning over new leaves
Stimulating conversation
A fine romance
The fruit of love
My dressing room
Perfume and fragrant
   thoughts
Nursery rhymes
Extravagance
Bits and bobs. Dibs and dabs.

Dare yourself the whim of giggles,
Spend a day with your silly dreams
Tickle your imagination . . .
Forever Play

Every other month, pick a day to
    celebrate something with a child:
Scrumpdillishicious day
Aqua Orange Pinklet
Hop Scotch, Willy Nilly, Tick Tock,
    Be Silly
Fantabulous Fairies Frolicking
Doting Dogs and Delightful
    Damsels
Grandeur Garden Games
Party Party Bo Barty Banana fana
    Mo Marty Party
Kiss, Kiss Make a Wish List
It's Raining Gumdrops
"Tell me Tootsie" Treasure Hunt
    Tuesday

Okay, so we let our imagination get the best of us here (cleaning up is a small price to pay), but impromptu occasions can be so much fun. To a child, unexpected experiences go a long way. Celebrate for the sake of celebration—the best excuse is no excuse at all.

Costumes always give plenty of chance for or show think an friends who succe ... well have much to be proud of.

Speak French when you can't think of the English for a thing— turn out your toes as you walk— and remember who you are.
—Lewis Carroll

A Page from my Journal

No One Knows
I Live Here...

documenting my
thoughts

3¢ U.S. POSTAGE
1876 COLORADO 1951
75TH ANNIVERSARY OF STATEHOOD

> Experience is not what happens to you; it is what you do with what happens to you.
> —Aldous Huxley

I enjoy journaling, documenting, and reflecting, having long since traded in my junior high dilemma diaries for a new kind of journal. This visual journal has become yet another forum for creating art. And why not? What thoughts inspire are as important as the thoughts themselves. Visual stimulation interests me, so my journal consists of both written words and beautiful images. It is another excuse to play rather than something else to "get to." I no longer feel pressured to write daily when events have not been monumental; I don't feel guilty when I don't write in my journal for days. The process of journaling has become an extension of something that I already love, like constructing a collage or painting a new design. Don't we all need more of what we love in our lives anyway?

Since each page of my journal is about making a pretty picture, there is no flow from beginning to end. I'm free to add to its pages at any time. A complete thought isn't necessary for this type of journal. How often does thinking about the outcome of a project stop us from starting the project in the first place?

The pages of my visual journal are decorated with drawings of my animals at play, delightful quotes, bits of art, and wonderful images. Something I see through my window might inspire many pages, and they may remain unfinished until weeks later. The evolution continues until my eyes are tickled by my own inspiration. The imagery in my journal has inspired a series of gift books; my sister-in-law, Annie, made us a lovely anniversary card inspired by my pages. The thoughtful card is tucked into my journal, adding to its splendor. One of my girlfriends used the concept to create a special family photo album. Perhaps a child's journal is not a book, but a lovely box that houses all of their favorite things or all of their discoveries from a special trip.

A living journal is one way to document or suspend in time the process of my thoughts. Instead of a family photo album, I have assembled on the bookshelves of my library a tribute to my relatives. Included are those I will never meet, alongside my siblings and grandparents. This living tribute contains my family history. I consider it living because it evolves with each new addition of family and friends. A living journal is quite personal and often revealing. I like to feel that my home is a living scrapbook. Tacked to a mirror in my dressing room is another form of living journal—the fragments of letters, momentos, postcards and photographs that commemorate a day's experience. A two-dimensional expression of what I call "creating altars."

When I invite people into my home, I have extended an invitation into my personal and private space. If they care to notice, they'll see how we spend our days whether in the garden, relaxed with feet up in front of the television, enjoying our animals, or preparing delicious food in our kitchen. They can see the quotes and words that have influenced our ways, our love of nature and fascination with business. Yes, if they are slightly observant, they might walk away from our home with a truer sense of the people who live in it. We have nothing to hide (except maybe the television, because I find it aesthetically hideous to look at) and we like our lives that way.

I often wonder when I visit other people's homes why they don't share themselves outwardly through their home. What is everybody so afraid of? Sure, I'm the first one to tuck the clutter behind cabinet doors, but not the memories and certainly not the loved ones.

Whether you create a journal to be inspired or to self-reflect, make it one that works for you.

134

134

134

俄羅斯木材出口下降

森林工業委員會主席
...森林工業委員會主席日前宣布，
...木材出口量今年
...
...今明年中溫可

星電子·固
進軍環求
年中溫可華興行

尚大會衝出亞洲
·固領導地位
衛星個人通訊

This Beaded Trim used in 1935

John and Tra
a tree K.I.C
first comes love
marage then Co

32

He Loves M

ages from my journal inspired by the rich gifts of romance and inspired by my darling, John Porter. My journal is my private playground, it's about creating pages of delicious layers, historic remnants, and tokens of what I love. Kind of like life—huh?

111

The Very idea of Ourselves....

CReating altars and collecting

Reflection, self-expression, the process of creation. We all practice these in our own way. In my case, there are many outlets for my outbursts of creativity. I need many options whether in my own home or designing for my business. In keeping with my need to transform my environment constantly, I create altars. My altars are collections of things assembled in a place where I can admire them. A dresser piled with lace, buttons, trims, ornate antique pins, cut glass perfume bottles, and velvet millinery flowers. Perhaps this three-dimensional collage is just an inspiration or perhaps it reminds me of who is dear to me. An altar might reflect discoveries from nature—a collage of a delicate bird's nest, bits of transparent sea glass, smooth pebbles, a tiny branch, a magnificent leaf or a sun-weathered shell found walking along the beach—all can be found on my altars.

My altars run the gamut from romantic to nostalgic, quirky to sentimental. Tiny spotlights on my mind's eye joined to my heart's desire.

An altar creates a space that is peaceful and quiet, yet thought-provoking. I am not in the habit of meditating but I definitely crave tranquil moments and time to reflect. My altars are not all in one room of my home but are sprinkled throughout. Sacred places for private thoughts. I am easily touched by a heartfelt token—the sentiment of a friend, a love note from my husband, a postcard from my parents' travels. In this busy life, I feel fortunate to know that someone has extended a kindness or taken time to handmake or handwrite something wonderful. Perhaps this is how my altars began. My pack rat tendencies took over and I suddenly couldn't throw anything away. These affectionate symbols deserve a special place, and my altars provide it. It's the handwritten tag with a quote from a friend, a fragment of handmade paper used to wrap a special gift, a quote I've read dozens of times but that continues to teach something new, a locket loved by my grandmother—all of these things I cherish, unthinkable to throw them away. So I stash them in a drawer until the proper opportunity strikes.

My altars often begin with my collections. I have a tendency to hoard things and before I know it, I have a collection. Collecting speaks to our passions and our whims. What is it that intrigues us about this thing or that thing? I can't explain it, but I know that I've felt it. The strongest urges usually come while standing in the crowd at an auction or browsing at a flea market. Some silly, special little thing speaks to me from under the rubble of junk and seizes my brain just long enough to convince me that if I don't drive away from this place with this special little thing waving happily from my back window, the consequences will be extreme, perhaps even severe. I admit, this actually happens to me and it happens to my friends, too! There's only one cure and that's to buy this special, silly little thing, not because it's worth anything or in perfect condition but because it tickles you in some funny way. It may not bring world peace or inner peace but you'll catch yourself smiling, even staring at it in your home. Repeat this episode a minimum of oh, let's say, ten to twelve times and you, my friend, can officially call yourself a collector.

A list of my current treasured collections:

Grandma Lucy's French lace
English lead farm animals
antique Halloween postcards
bric-a-brac, tassels and trims
framed specimens of exotic butterflies
   and insects
delicate tea cups
old and delicious books
vintage linens
tarnished but detailed silver
antique dolls
perfume
shoes (especially of the python variety)
dinnerware
glassware
even a Pez dispenser collection

You'll find my collections proudly displayed for their charm and slightly imperfect character throughout my home. Treasures that take me back to the days when I discovered them find interchangeable places within my walls. These collections are the not-so-blank canvasses for many of my altars; new treasures to hold the contents of my vignetted memories and cherished objects.

Build an altar or collection around a favorite color, a particular theme or season. I sometimes like to shut my collections away so that when they are pulled out again, it's like seeing friends you haven't visited in a while. There are many philosophies on how to assemble a collection. Some antique collectors specialize in the vintage, condition, rarity, and value of a thing as the main consideration for buying. And while all collectors feel passionate about their treasures, I particularly enjoy the history of my things. I don't usually base a purchase on dollar value—a ding or two rarely keeps me from adding to my collection. Variety is truly the spice of life.

An assemblage of treasures for the sheer delight they bring. A slice of your childhood, a memory in the making, or mementos of shared celebrations. An altar may be misunderstood even by those who are nearest and dearest. There is no need to define for anyone but yourself when assembling an altar.

My friend Maura says that she carries an altar in her pocket. All of the tiny things that catch her eye during the day, she scoops up and adds to her collection. At day's end, her altar spills onto her nightstand, where it rests only to return to a new pocket the following day. She keeps adding to it until her pockets overflow. Her growing altar now lives in the dresser drawer. Whatever your version of an altar, the way it warms your heart is what's special. For some, it's the traditional ritual of dressing a tree each holiday season with treasures collected or given by loved ones, or the fragments of a destroyed collection of antique dishes transformed into a stunning and intricate mosaic mirror. The concept of the altar is not new; perhaps you unknowingly possess one?

Stay open to every delight, whim, and fancy!

Collections are the remnants of our existence. Revealing of the character and all that beckoned her. Our collections linger beyond our years.

POST CARD

All the World's Memory

This time, like all times, is a very good one—
if we but know what to do with it.

—Emerson

The walls of your home contain the sum of your life experiences. All the memories are stored here, your permanent record. Loves gained, loves lost, family secrets, social gatherings, unspoken truths, shared relationships. So many layers of experience to be recalled. Our house wears its memories on its doors, floors, and walls. Cherish the chips, dents, and cracks, for these are the places where character lives.

What could be more fabulous than the familiar and delicious comfort of home? Take your coat off and stay a while.

The lives we lead in our private homes don't necessarily reflect the lives of its former dwellers. We each experience home in vastly different ways, and our lifestyle determines the experience. Some days home is about sanctuary, a place to nestle in and relax. Other days, home is chaos—everybody tending to their hectic schedules, trying to meet the day's demands. Your home has as many faces as you wish. What people see through the windows might not really reflect the lives actually lived there.

Over time, preserve what is precious about your home—a growth chart running up the wall or a collage of the phone numbers of loved ones scribbled on the inside of a kitchen cabinet door. Some things are meant to be saved—don't be tempted to discard something that might be lost forever. I salvaged from my parents' home some prints of French ladies that hung on my childhood bedroom wall. Not in my wildest dreams could I imagine parting with the broken bed that was slept on by five generations of our family. Its solid veneer is battered and worn and we haven't had a guest yet who hasn't banged into its obtrusive foot board. Fair warning is given when guests arrive: You'll bang your head on the chandelier, which is hung too low, and you'll crack your shin on the bed. Despite the mishaps it causes, this precious keepsake will remain a beloved fixture in our home.

Is this not a precious home? Is it not
worth our love? Does it not deserve
all the inventiveness and courage and
generosity of which we are capable . . . ?
—Barbara Ward
(1914–1981)

Our domain tells the story of the humble beginnings of our journey, nurturing a marriage and raising a business. I'm reminded in my home of my own family, who encouraged me to listen to my own voice. Setting up home has taught me the lessons of when to humbly accept our nest and when to boldly change the face of it. The spirit of home speaks to our hearts and fondly recalls our memories. Holidays and their seasons are marked with the passing of time.

Home provides shared celebrations with family and a place to entertain friends. As a place for solitude, it's the sanctuary where you can reflect and be inspired. Our homes give us the opportunity to express our style. Mine leads me to the splendor of nature that awaits outside our door. A house stands patient, sturdy, and still while the journey of our

lifetime unfolds and it will remain for others long after we are gone.

Like life, home will be what you make of it. We borrow from what we know and trust; our parents' habits, childhood experiences, family memories, and suggestions of friends. After all is said and done, we bake our own cake. We add a pinch of ourselves and stir in a good deal of our own expectations, realities, decisions, and passions. Stir it all up, sift through the likes and dislikes. Pour in the values, rituals, and traditions and then bake happily on high.